Extreme Privilege

Changing Your World through Prayer

Written/Compiled by
Dr. John Sparks

Editor
Larry Weeden

PK PROMISE KEEPERS ®
MEN OF INTEGRITY

Denver, Colorado

P.O. Box 103001
Denver, CO 80250-3001

Contents

Chapter 1

A Message from Bill McCartney

———◆·◆·◆———

O n December 19, 1891, E.M. Bounds, the great prophet of prayer, wrote: "Revival begins in prayer. The prayerful spirit is the spirit of revival. The spirit of supplicating prayer is the pledge of revival, its harbinger and source. The revival begins in prayer, continues by prayer, and if it ends well, ends in prayer. The revival always begins with mighty prayer. The number praying may be few. The pastor alone may be carrying the burden of a broken heart and crying to God in his penitence, sighs, and tears. The praying ones may be a small circle, but whether the praying ones be pastor or people, the circle of prayer is always the center of revival."

Before every revival in history, God did two things: He placed in the hearts of His people a hunger for Himself, and He poured out upon them a spirit of prayer.

Throughout history, a new thirst for God has always awakened a new interest in prayer and fasting:

Moses prayed and fasted 40 days before he received the Ten Commandments.

Jehoshaphat "feared, and set himself to seek the LORD, and proclaimed a fast throughout all Judah" (2 Chronicles 20:3, KJV).

David "wept, and chastened [his] soul with fasting" (Psalm 69:10, KJV).

Since the day of Pentecost, every time the church has lost her power and authority, God has touched down in revival power upon His people. Every revival has begun, not with an earthshaking, sin-scorching visitation of the Spirit of

1

God, but with a desire of God's people to fast and pray for a renewal of His church.

Today, the hour is critical. America is in the greatest moral and spiritual crisis in her history! Many in the church have left their first love and have failed to be a holy people. God demands holiness! He will not allow us to go on with dirty lives, in lethargy and unconcern!

One pastor said recently, "During our Wednesday evening service, ... the Lord released a prayer burden from heaven... This time of intense, overwhelming travail for our nation lasted for three and one-half hours. During that time, I wept off and on, harder than I ever knew was possible."

I long for a burden like that. I want to weep harder than I ever thought possible. I long for a sense of desperation about the need of our nation. I yearn for a new hunger for God; for a desperation for a touch from His hand; for a longing for closer fellowship with Him; and for an insatiable desire for the power of God upon His clergy.

As Leonard Ravenhill wrote years ago, in words even more appropriate for today, "This is the time to blush that we have no shame. This is the time to weep for our lack of tears, the time to bend low that we have lost the humble touch of servants, the time to groan that we have no burden, the time to be angry with ourselves that we have no anger over the devil's monopoly in the end time hour, the time to chastise ourselves that the world can get along so easily with us and not attempt to chastise us."

Who is responsible for the pitiful state of our nation? The millions of unborn babies who have had their lives violently taken from them? The thousands of criminals who make the streets of most of our cities a war zone? The hundreds of thousands of souls passing into eternity without hope every day? *The church is responsible!*

Because we have failed to take a stand against sin. We have failed to fast and pray for God to intervene. And we act as if we really don't care. Our attitude has been,"If it doesn't touch my home or my family, who cares?"

> 200,000 souls a day are passing
> one by one away
> in Christless guilt and gloom,
> without one ray of hope or light
> with future dark as endless night,
> they're passing to their doom.
> Oh Church of God,
> what will you say
> when in that awful judgment day
> they charge you with their doom?

Where do we place the responsibility for revival? "Judgment must begin at the house of God" (1 Peter 4:17, KJV).

Here are the issues:

God wants the hearts of His people to be broken. "The sacrifices of God are a broken spirit: a broken and a contrite heart" (Psalm 51:17, KJV).

God longs for His people to mourn over the sin in their lives, in their communities, and in our nation. The prophet Jeremiah wrote,"Oh that my head were waters, and mine eyes a fountain of tears" (Jeremiah 9:1, KJV). Why are our eyes so dry? Because our hearts are dry! Why are we so blind? Why can't we see the vision of death when we look at the condition of our cities? Our inner cities go unreached, and the urban man is untouched!

God longs for His people to hunger and thirst after Him. "I will pour water upon him that is thirsty, and floods upon the dry ground" (Isaiah 44:3, KJV). "If any man is thirsty, let him come to Me and drink. He who believes in Me, as the Scripture said,'From his innermost being shall flow rivers of living water'" (John 7:37-38, NASB).

Oh, for a heart that is burdened!
Infused with a passion to pray;
Oh, for a stirring within me!
Oh for His power each day.
Oh, for a heart like my Savior,
who being in agony prayed;
such caring for others, Lord give me;
on my heart let burdens be laid.
My Father, I long for this passion!
To pour out myself for the lost;
to lay down my life to save others;
to pray, whatever the cost.
Lord, teach me, oh teach me this secret,
I'm hungry this lesson to learn;
This passionate passion for others,
for this blessing, dear Jesus, I yearn.
Father, this lesson I long for from Thee!
Oh, let Thy Spirit reveal this to me.

O God, send revival, and let it begin in me.

Action Points As You Read This Booklet

1. Allow the Lord to draw you closer to Himself. It may
    be uncomfortable at first; you likely will feel exposed and
    vulnerable. Wait, seek, repent, and prepare to be used in
    new ways.
2. Let your spirit be nurtured through the various chapters.
    Some contain deep truths that will need to be read and
    studied again and again.
3. Pass this booklet along throughout your whole church.
    You will notice that the pastor, staff, and their families are
    the focus of intercession. Start with blessing and support-
    ing them, and then pray those same requests for your own
    family and others. God wants to transform your church
    from the top down and from the inside out.
4. Remember that there is no more valuable productive
    way to spend time than on your knees before Almighty
    God. That is *the* best place to begin changing your world.

Chapter 2

Touching the Heart of God

"Dad, I'm so hungry. May I have some bread?"

Does that sound like prayer to you? Or is it more like a child asking his father for what he needs? God invites us to come to Him like little children. It's as simple as saying, "Daddy, I need you."

God holds the key to all your longings: provision, protection, belonging, compassion, forgiveness. And He wants to provide them for you—just ask Him. He strengthens and encourages you and your church family through faith in the Lord Jesus Christ. Prayer—corporate prayer—is the power source from which that faith derives its life. Church families that pray together lay hold of the very power of God to cope with the challenges of daily living.

This guide contains a bundle of suggestions and helpful resources. It offers practical, motivating ideas and encouragement designed to help church families unite and witness the power of God. You'll see that prayer is really quite simple and that it is the single-most-important experience your church family can share.

Prayer can be as dynamic and varied as your imagination and creativity. Prayers can be spoken aloud, sung, staged, danced, or even painted. The possibilities are endless as you turn your church family's heart toward the Lord.

God wants your church family to shine like lights in a rapidly darkening and dysfunctional world. He desires each member to have his eyes open to realities that others refuse to see. He longs for you to walk with Christ through a larger, more wondrous world than some are capable of imagining. Take the roof off and establish a direct link between your church and the heart of the King of all creation.

Adapted by permission from The Power of Family Prayer, *copyright © 1999 National Day of Prayer.*

Chapter 3

Extreme Results

C oaches get extreme results from players who are willing to pay any price for victory. If pastors and Christian leaders could tap into that same kind of commitment to the cause, our churches and ministries would all be championship teams for Christ!

The late Green Bay Packers coach Vince Lombardi wrote, "A man can be as great as he wants to be. If you ... have the courage and determination, the dedication, and the competitive drive, and are willing to sacrifice ... and pay the price for the things that are worthwhile, it can be done." He continued, "I firmly believe that any man's finest hour, the greatest fulfillment of all that he holds dear, is that moment when he has worked his heart out in a good cause and lies exhausted on the field of battle—victorious."

What a goal! To lie exhausted on the field of battle— victorious. You can be great for God, and for far more than an earthly prize. "I press on toward the goal to win the prize for which God has called me" (Philippians 3:14, NIV). "Do you not know that in a race all the runners run, but only one gets the prize? Run in such a way as to get the prize. Everyone who competes in the games goes into strict training. They do it to get a crown that will not last; but we do it to get a crown that will last forever" (1 Corinthians 9:24-25, NIV). Want extreme results from your Christian life? Set your eyes on the prize!

In the days of the Roman Empire, 40 Christian soldiers were serving in one of the Roman legions. The army was involved in a campaign in the high mountains of northern Armenia. It was a bitterly cold winter. Then the emperor issued a decree to his generals: "Every soldier must march past a statue of the emperor, do obeisance, pour out a libation of wine, and drop incense on the fire."

At the appointed time, the trumpets blew and the Roman legion (12,000 soldiers) bowed down, poured out a libation of wine, dropped the incense, and worshipped the emperor. But those 40 Christians—wrestlers by training, renowned for their prowess on the field of battle and their triumphs in the amphitheater and the athletic games—refused to bow and worship the emperor.

Their general begged them to obey, and for a moment they hesitated. Then their leader announced, "For Rome we will fight on any field, under any sky. If necessary, we will even die in our service to the emperor. But we will worship no one save Jesus Christ our master."

The general pronounced sentence upon them. They were to be stripped naked and marched onto a frozen lake. There they sang: "Forty wrestlers, wrestling for Thee, O Christ, claim for Thee the victory and from Thee the crown." One by one they froze to death, the sound of their song becoming fainter and fainter.

Finally, one of the wrestlers stood shivering before the tent of the general and declared, "I will do obeisance! I will pour the wine! I will burn the incense!"

The sentinel at the general's tent, although a pagan, was stirred by the heroic faith of the other wrestlers. He answered, "Since you proved to be a coward, I will take your place." Stripped of his armor and clothing, he was marched onto the lake. For a time the soldiers around their campfires could hear a solitary voice singing, "Forty wrestlers, wrestling for Thee, O Christ, claim for Thee the victory and from Thee the crown."

When the sun rose over the bleak Armenian mountains the next morning, it looked down upon 40 men who had died for Christ and received from Him an eternal crown.

There is no greater prize in this life than to know that you stood for something. If you can stand before God in the place of others; if you can charge the battlements of the enemy on behalf of your pastor, your church, your family, and your community; if you can endure hardship as a good soldier for Christ; then you can say with the apostle Paul, "I have fought the good fight, I have finished the race, I have kept the faith. Now there is in store for me the crown of righteousness, which the Lord, the righteous Judge, will award to me on that day" (2 Timothy 4:7-8, NIV).

You can do all of that while on your knees in prayer to the Lord.

Chapter 4

Why Pray?

———◆◆◆———

There are numerous reasons why we should pray. The following Scripture passages address a number of those reasons. Read through them, and as you do so, underline the verses in your Bible to remind you of why you ought to pray.

1. The Bible instructs us to pray. This is the primary reason we pray.
    *   Matthew 5:44
    *   Matthew 6:6
    *   Romans 12:12
    *   1 Thessalonians 5:17
    *   James 5:16

2. Jesus prayed regularly. We should follow His example.
    *   Luke 3:21; 5:16; 6:12; 9:18, 28; 11:1
    *   John 17

3. Prayer is how we communicate with God. Through prayer, we can worship and praise God, confess our sins, and repent of them. We can also submit our requests, learn God's will, and seek His help.
    *   Philippians 4:6
    *   1 Thessalonians 5:16-18

4. Through prayer, God allows us to participate in His works. Prayer plays a part in bringing others to faith in Christ. Prayer can heal nations and grant us strength to endure trials.
    *   2 Chronicles 7:14
    *   Matthew 9:37-38
    *   Colossians 4:3-4
    *   Hebrews 4:15-16

5.   Prayer gives us power over evil. Physical strength is
      of no use in the spiritual realm. But even the physically
      weak can be strong in prayer.
      • Matthew 26:41
      • Mark 9:29
      • 1 Timothy 4:8

6.   Prayer is always available to us. Nothing can keep the
      believer from coming before God in prayer. Nations
      may condemn and forbid God's Word, but prayer is
      unstoppable.
      • Psalm 139:7
      • Romans 8:38-39

7.   Prayer keeps us humble before God. Through prayer
      we realize that God is in control and we can do
      nothing apart from Him.
      • Jeremiah 32:17
      • John 15:5
      • Romans 8:28

8.   Prayer grants us the privilege of experiencing God.
      Prayer gives us an experiential basis for our faith.
      • Genesis 18:1-33
      • John 14:16-17

9.   Answered prayer has the potential to be an incredible
      witness to unbelievers. Skeptics will always have criti-
      cisms and doubts regarding answered prayer, but some
      will see the power of God at work and, as a result, may
      be drawn to Christ.
      • Colossians 4:3
      • James 5:16

10.   Prayer strengthens the bonds between believers.
      Scripture instructs us to pray for and confess our sins
      to one another. Through this process, we come to
      better understand the needs of others and are able to
      empathize with them.

- James 5:16
- 1 John 5:15-16

11.   Prayer can succeed where other means have failed. Prayer is not a last resort, but it can often make a difference when other methods have failed.
- 1 Chronicles 16:11
- James 5:13-15

Adapted by permission from The Power of Family Prayer, *copyright © 1999 National Day of Prayer.*

Chapter 5

Praying Men

by E.M. Bounds

———◆———

P rayer is the mightiest agent to advance God's work.
Only praying hearts and hands can do God's work.
Prayer succeeds when all else fails. Prayer has won great
victories and rescued, with notable triumph, God's saints
when every hope was gone. Men who know how to pray are
the greatest boon God can give to earth. They are the richest
gift earth can offer heaven. Men who know how to use this
weapon of prayer are God's best soldiers, His mightiest
leaders.

Praying men are God's chosen leaders. The distinction
between the leaders that God brings to the front to lead and
bless His people and those leaders who owe their position of
leadership to worldly, selfish, unsanctified selection is this:
God's leaders are preeminently men of prayer. Prayer distin-
guishes them and is the simple, divine attestation of their call,
the seal of their separation by God. Whatever other graces or
gifts they may have, the gift and grace of prayer towers above
them all. In whatever else they may share or differ, in the gift
of prayer they are one.

What would God's leaders be without prayer? Strip Moses
of his power in prayer, a gift that made him eminent in pagan
estimate, and the crown is taken from his head, the food and
fire of his faith are gone. Elijah, without his praying, would
have neither record nor place in the divine legation. His life
would be insipid, cowardly, its energy, defiance, and fire gone.
Without Elijah's praying, the Jordan would never have yielded
to the stroke of his mantle, nor would the stern angel of death
have honored him with the chariot and horses of fire.

The argument that God uses to quiet Ananias's fears and

convince him of Paul's condition and sincerity: "Behold,
he prayeth." This was the epitome of Paul's history, the
basis for his life and work. Paul, Luther, Wesley—what
would these chosen ones of God be without the distin-
guishing and controlling element of prayer? They were
leaders for God because they were mighty in prayer. They
were not leaders because of their brilliance, their inex-
haustible resources, their magnificent cultured or native
environment. They were leaders because they could
command the power of God by the power of prayer.
Praying men are not just men who say prayers or men who
pray by habit. Praying men are men with whom prayer is a
mighty force, an energy that moves heaven and pours
untold treasures of good on earth.

Praying men are the men who spend much time with
God. Praying men always feel a great need and desire to be
alone with God. Though very busy men, they always stop
at some appointed time for communion with God. They
have spent much time alone with Him and have found that
the secret of wise and powerful leadership for God is in
these seasons of special access and grace.

Praying men are the men of the single eye. They have
been so much alone with God, have seen so much of His
glory, have learned so much of His will, have been fash-
ioned so strongly after His image, that He fixes and fills
their gaze. All else is too insignificant to engage their
attention, too little to catch their eye. A double vision—
one for self and the other for God—mightily hinders
prayer.

Praying men are men of one book; they feed of God's
Word; it lives in them in vitalizing force and abides in them
in full authority and faith. They are Bible men. The Bible
inspires their prayers and quickens their faith. They rest
upon its promises as on a globe of granite.

Praying men are the only productive workers for God.
True prayer is a working force, a divine energy that must
come out, that is too strong to be still. The work of praying
men achieves the best results because it is done by God's
energy. Praying men have His direction to do His work for
His glory, under the full and cheering beam of His presence, His Word, and His Spirit.

Praying men serve to protect the church from the materialism that affects all its plans and polity and hardens its lifeblood. A secret, deadly poison circulates, convincing the church that it need not be so dependent on purely spiritual forces as it used to be. Changed times and changed conditions have brought it out of its spiritual straits and dependencies and put it where other forces can bear it to its climax. A fatal snare of this kind has lured the church into worldly embraces, dazzled her leaders, weakened her foundations, and deprived her of much of her beauty and strength.

Praying men save the church from this material tendency. They pour into it the original spiritual forces. They lift it from the sandbars of materialism and press it out into the ocean depths of spiritual power. Praying men keep God in the church full force. They keep His hand on the helm as He trains the church in strength and trust.

The number and efficiency of the laborers in God's vineyard in all lands are dependent on the men of prayer. By the divinely arranged process, the number and success of the consecrated laborers depend on the power of prayer. Prayer opens wide the doors of access, prepares the laborer to enter, and gives holy boldness, firmness, and fruit.

Praying men are needed in all fields of spiritual labor. There is no position, high or low, in the church of God that can be well filled without prayer. There is no position where Christians are found that does not demand a faith that always prays and never faints. Praying men are needed in the house of business as well as the house of God that they may order and direct trade, not according to the maxims of this world, but according to biblical precepts and the maxims of the heavenly life.

Men of prayer are needed especially in the positions of church influence, honor, and power. The leaders of church thought, church work, and church life should be men of signal power in prayer. It is the praying heart that sanctifies the toil and skill of the hands and the toil and wisdom of the head. Prayer keeps work aligned with God's will and keeps thought aligned with God's Word. The

solemn responsibilities of leadership in God's church, in a
large or limited sphere, should be so hedged about with
prayer that between it and the world there would be an
impassable gulf. Leaders should be so elevated and puri-
fied by prayer that neither cloud nor night would stain the
radiance or dim the sight of a constant meridian view of
God.

Many church leaders seem to think that if they can be
prominent as men of thought, of plans, of scholarly attain-
ments, of eloquent gifts and conspicuous activities, that
these are enough and will atone for the absence of the
higher spiritual power that comes from much prayer. But
these are vain and paltry in the serious business of bringing glory to God, controlling the church for Him, and
bringing it into full accord with its divine mission.

Praying men are the men who have done so much for
God in the past. They are the ones who have won the
victories for God and spoiled His foes. They are the ones
who have set up His kingdom in the very camps of His
enemies. There are no other conditions for success today.
The nineteenth century has not suspended the necessity
or force of prayer. [Nor has the twenty-first.] There is no
substitute by which its gracious ends can be secured. Only
praying hands can build for God. Men of prayer are God's
mighty ones on the earth, His master builders. They may
be destitute of all else, but with the wrestlings and
prevailings of a simple-hearted faith they are mighty—the
mightiest force for God. Church leaders may be gifted in
all else, but without this greatest of gifts they are as
Samson shorn of his locks, or as the altars of the temple
where heavenly flame has died without the divine
presence.

Adapted by permission from E.M. Bounds, The Weapon
of Prayer *(Baker Book House).*

Chapter 6

Prayer Promises

- 2 Chronicles 7:14 *"If my people, who are called by my name, will humble themselves and pray and seek my face and turn from their wicked ways, then will I hear from heaven and will forgive their sin and will heal their land"* (NIV).
- Psalm 145:18-19 *"The LORD is near to all who call upon Him, to all who call upon Him in truth. He will fulfill the desire of those who fear Him; He will also hear their cry and will save them"* (NASB). Proverbs 15:8b *"The prayer of the upright is His delight"* (NASB).
- Isaiah 65:24 *"It shall come to pass, that before they call, I will answer: and while they are yet speaking, I will hear"* (KJV).
- Jeremiah 33:3 *"Call to Me, and I will answer you, and show you great and mighty things, which you do not know"* (NKJV).
- Mark 11:24 *"Whatever things you ask when you pray, believe that you receive them, and you will have them"* (NKJV).
- John 14:13-14 *"And whatever you ask in My name, that will I do, that the Father may be glorified in the Son. If you ask Me anything in My name, I will do it"* (NASB).
- John 15:7 *"If you abide in Me, and My words abide in you, you will ask what you desire, and it shall be done for you"* (NKJV).
- John 16:23b,24b *"Whatever you ask the Father in My name He will give you. ... Ask, and you will receive, that your joy may be full"* (NKJV).
- Romans 8:26 *"Likewise the Spirit also helps in our weaknesses. For we do not know what we should pray for as we ought, but the Spirit Himself makes intercession for us with groanings which cannot be uttered"* (NKJV).

- 1 Peter 3:12 *"For the eyes of the Lord are on the righteous, and His ears are open to their prayers" (NKJV).*
- 1 John 5:14-15 *"Now this is the confidence that we have in Him, that if we ask anything according to His will, He hears us. And if we know that He hears us, whatever we ask, we know that we have the petitions that we have asked of Him" (NKJV).*

Awesome Power

- Prayer binds the devil and his bands of demons.
- Prayer unleashes the powers of heaven.
- Prayer blesses God and His children.
- Prayer releases the angelic hosts to do their work in ministering to the heirs of salvation.
- Prayer changes the destinies of nations and sets men free.
- Prayer breaks the spell of Satan over individual lives.
- Prayer is the exertion of spiritual authority over the invisible war that is raging.
- Prayer is our becoming one with God.

Chapter 7

How to Pray

———◆———

A homeowner seeking a gardener reviewed the following letter of recommendation: "John Smith is an excellent gardener! He knows exactly when to plant. He is very good at knowing when, what type, and how much fertilizer to use. He knows when to water, when to prune, when to cultivate, and when to harvest. He knows everything to do … *but he won't!*"

Does that sound like our praying?

> We want God's power in our lives, and we know how to appropriate it.
>
> We want God's will to be done in our lives, and we know how to find it.
>
> We want to see our loved ones come to Christ, and we know how to win them.
>
> We want to see unity in the Body of Christ, and we know how to attain it.
>
> We want our church blessed, and we know what to do.
>
> We want to see our pastor filled with God's revival power, and we know how to pray for him.
>
> We want to see the blessings of God upon our families, and we know how to get them.
>
> We know how to ask God for all these things … *but we won't!*

I often say my prayers, but do I really pray?
And do the wishes of my heart go with the words I say?
I may as well kneel down and worship gods of stone,
As to offer to the living God a prayer of words alone.

For words without the heart, the Lord will never hear,
Nor will He to those lips attend whose prayer is not sincere.
Lord, show me what I need, and teach me how to pray,
And help me when I seek Thy grace to mean the words I say.

In Luke 11, the disciples came to Jesus with a request:
"Lord, teach us to pray!" In response, Jesus gave them and us a
model prayer. The great theologian John Calvin said, "We ought
to examine our prayers by this rule." As the Ten Commandments were written by the finger of God to give the moral law
of the universe; as the Lord personally dictated the pattern for
the tabernacle and the temple; as Jesus gave us the rules for
living the Christian life in the Beatitudes; so Jesus also gave us
the pattern for prayer in the Lord's Prayer (which might be
better titled the Disciple's Prayer). It is clear, concise, and
complete.

A False Way and a True Way

In Matthew 6, we are reminded that there's a false way to
pray and a true way to pray. The essential fault of false prayer
is that it centers on the one praying rather than the One to
whom the prayer is directed. Jesus explained, "And when you
pray, you shall not be like the hypocrites. For they love to pray
standing in the synagogues and on the corners of the streets,
that they may be seen by men. Assuredly, I say to you, they
have their reward" (Matthew 6:5, NKJV).

When the Pharisees went to the temple to pray, they stood
in a visible place so everyone could see. But Jesus pointed out,
in contrast, a tax collector who stood afar off, could not even
lift his eyes to heaven, and cried out, "God, be merciful to me a
sinner!" (Luke 18:13, NKJV). Jesus said that tax collector went
to his house justified, because "he who humbles himself will be
exalted" (verse 14).

False prayer is demonstrated by repetitive praying. The
Lord's Prayer in Matthew 6 can be said in 15 seconds. A large
congregation can say it in less than 30 seconds. It is estimated
that 500 million people in the world can say those 66 words
(in the KJV) from memory. But do we really understand that

those words were meant for praying, not just for saying? Merely mouthing words over and over falls into the category of "vain repetitions" (Matthew 6:7). Or, as Shakespeare's Hamlet put it, "My words fly up, my thoughts remain below, words without thought never to heaven go."

There is, however, a true way to pray. It starts with several prerequisites.

The first prerequisite is *exclusion.* We must get alone with, and focus exclusively on, the living God, losing ourselves in Him. "Enter into thy closet," Jesus said in Matthew 6:6 (KJV). That indicates a private place. Then He instructed, "Shut thy door," which means we shut out the world and its cares. In other words, we need to find a place where we won't be disturbed, where we can get alone with God, away from the distractions of life. The person who is willing to shut himself up with God will see Him and touch Him in a real way.

The second prerequisite is *realization.* We must realize we are coming into the presence of an awesome God. We approach our prayer closet with this thought: *I am now entering into the throne room of the King of kings, the Lord of lords, the almighty, eternal, great God, with all His power and might and majesty; a God who is a "consuming fire" (Deuteronomy 4:24, NKJV); a God who is all light, and "in Him is no darkness at all" (1 John 1:5, NKJV); the absolute, holy God who is the sovereign creator of the universe and yet who is also "our Father!"* We realize, too, that He "is able to do exceedingly abundantly above all that we ask or think" (Ephesians 3:20, NKJV).

A third prerequisite in the prayer process is *confidence.* "Now this is the confidence that we have in Him, that if we ask anything according to His will, He hears us. And if we know that He hears us, whatever we ask, we know that we have the petitions that we have asked of Him" (1 John 5:14-15, NKJV). "All things, whatever you ask in prayer, believing, you will receive" (Matthew 21:22, NKJV). "Whatever things you ask when you pray, believe that you receive them, and you will have them" (Mark 11:24, NKJV). "All things are possible to him who believes" (Mark 9:23, NKJV).

Posture, Place, and Time

In His "Disciple's Prayer," Jesus did not teach us the posture of prayer. The posture of our hearts is what really matters. "Humble yourselves in the sight of the Lord, and He will lift you up" (James 4:10, NKJV). People in the Bible prayed while standing, sitting, kneeling, lying down, bowing, lifting their hands, lifting their eyes, placing their heads between their knees, and pounding on their chests.

Nor did Jesus specify where to pray. People in the Bible prayed during battles, in caves, in closets, in a garden, on the mountainside, by a river, by the sea, in the street, in God's house, in bed, in a home, on a housetop, in prison, in solitude, in the wilderness, in a fish, and on a cross.

Jesus didn't teach us when to pray, either. The Bible shows us people praying in the early morning, midmorning, at evening, three times a day, before meals, after meals, at the ninth hour, at bedtime, at midnight, day and night, often, when they were young, when they were old, when in trouble, every day, and always.

Nor did Jesus tell us what to wear or how to act during prayer. Looking again at the Bible, we see that people wore sackcloth, sat in ashes, shaved their heads, cried out, put dust on their heads, tore their clothes, fasted, groaned, sighed, wept, sweat blood, agonized with broken hearts and broken spirits, poured out their hearts, made oaths, offered sacrifices, offered praise, and sang.

Elements of Prayer

However, wherever, and whenever we pray, prayer should incorporate certain elements. These include:

Loving praise: "I will bless the LORD at all times; His praise shall continually be in my mouth" (Psalm 34:1, NKJV). "O Lord, open my lips, and my mouth shall show forth Your praise" (Psalm 51:15, NKJV).

Gratitude: "I will sacrifice to You with the voice of thanksgiving" (Jonah 2:9, NKJV). When the day comes that we have nothing more to ask for, we will have everything to be thankful for.

A sense of reverential awe toward God's holiness:
The Hebrews did not treat God as if He were a man. They
realized that when they prayed, they were face-to-face
with a holy God. "Woe is me, for I am undone! Because I
am a man of unclean lips, and I dwell in the midst of a
people of unclean lips; for my eyes have seen the King, the
LORD of Hosts" (Isaiah 6:5, NKJV).

A spirit of obedience: "We ought to obey God rather
than men" (Acts 5:29, NKJV). "Behold, to obey is better
than sacrifice" (1 Samuel 15:22, NKJV). "The LORD our God
we will serve, and His voice we will obey" (Joshua 24:24,
NKJV). The true believer goes to God with no reservations
and with a spirit of obedience, desiring to please Him.

Confession of sin: "Who may ascend into the hill of the
LORD? Or who may stand in His holy place? He who has
clean hands and a pure heart, who has not lifted up his
soul to an idol, nor sworn deceitfully" (Psalm 24:3-4,
NKJV).

Unselfishness: Most of us come to the Lord with a lot
of "Gimmee, gimmee, gimmee! Me, me, me! I want! I
need!" However, you will find no first-person singular
pronouns in the Lord's Prayer. Instead it's "Our Father ...
our daily bread ... our debts ... our debtors ... Your name ...
Your kingdom ... Your will." Prayer is always unselfish! We
ought to be asking one another, "What do *you* need? How
can I pray for *you?*"

Perseverance: Never give up! Nehemiah fasted and
prayed for four to five months. "So it was, when I heard
these words, that I sat down and wept, and mourned for
many days; I was fasting and praying before the God of
heaven" (Nehemiah 1:4, NKJV). Many believers have seen
loved ones come to faith in Christ only after years and
even decades of faithful praying.

Humility: "Blessed are the poor in spirit" (Matthew
5:3). "Walk worthy ... with all lowliness and gentleness,
with longsuffering, bearing with one another in love"
(Ephesians 4:1-2, NKJV).

Chapter 8

Prayerless Praying

by E.M. Bounds

━━━◆━◆━

There is much prayerless praying. The attitude and semblance of prayer are in it, but there is no real praying, no projecting of the desires with vigor and in a flame to heaven. The form and show are seen, but the substance and being of prayer are entirely absent. Prayers have been said, the performance gone through, but no real praying has been done. As far as any real benefit is secured, turning the crank of a praying machine would have done as well.

Prayerless prayers are not only a perversion, a waste, and a delusion, but they manufacture unbelievers by the score. They get no answers and produce no gracious results. They are vain performances, and others recognize their emptiness and barren results. Men hear of prodigious benefits secured by prayer, of the matchless good promised in God's Word to prayer, and they mark at once the great gulf between the results promised and results realized. ...

Prayerless praying lacks the essential element of true praying; it is not based on desire and is devoid of earnestness and faith. Desire burdens the chariot of prayer, and faith drives its wheels.

Prayerless praying has no burden because there is no sense of need; there is no ardency because there is no vision, strength, or glow of faith. There is no mighty pressure to pray, no holding on to God with the relentless despairing grasp, "I will not let Thee go, except Thou bless me." There is no utter self-abandon, lost in the throes of a desperate, pertinacious, and consuming plea, "Yet now, if Thou wilt forgive their sin; and if not, blot me, I pray Thee, out of Thy book," or, "Give me Scotland or I die."

Prayerless praying stakes nothing on the issue, for it has nothing to stake. It comes with empty hands, indeed, but they are listless hands as well as empty. They have never learned the lesson of empty hands clinging to the cross; this lesson to them has no form or comeliness.

Prayerless praying has no heart in its praying. The lack of heart knocks the bottom out of praying and makes it empty. Heart, soul, and life must be in our praying; the heavens must feel the force of our crying in order to have sympathy for our bitter and needy state. A need that oppresses us, and has no relief but in our crying to God, must be voiced through praying.

Prayerless praying is insincere. It has no honesty because we express in words what we do not really want in heart. Our prayers give formal utterance to things for which our hearts are not only not hungry, but for which they really have no taste. We heard that eminent and saintly preacher, now in heaven, Dr. Jefferson Hamilton, speak abruptly and sharply to a congregation that had just risen from prayer with the question and statement, "What did you pray for? If God should take hold of you and shake you and demand what you prayed for, you could not tell Him to save your life what the prayer was that has just died from your lips." So it always is, prayerless praying has neither memory nor heart. A mere form, a heterogeneous mass, an insipid compound, a mixture thrown together for its sound, but with neither heart nor aim, is prayerless praying. A dry routine, a dreary drudge, a dull and heavy task is this prayerless praying.

But prayerless praying is much worse than either task or drudge; it divorces praying from living. It utters its words against the world but with heart and life runs into the world. It prays for humility but nurtures pride; it prays for self-denial while indulging the flesh. In gracious results, nothing exceeds true praying, but better not to pray at all than to pray prayerless prayers, for they are but sinning, and the worst of sinning is to sin on our knees.

✠

Reflecting on Bounds's words, have you found yourself leaving prayer time thinking, *Did I really get hold of God?* Do you sometimes wonder if we really pray because we have a passion for God and long to come into His presence with a great sense of need to talk to Him? How much of our praying is prayerless praying? How often do we pray so others will hear us, or as a duty or an obligation? How much do we hunger and thirst for God?

"As the deer pants for the water brooks, so pants my soul for You, O God. My soul thirsts for God, for the living God" (Psalm 42:1-2, NKJV).

"O God, You are my God; early will I seek You; my soul thirsts for You; my flesh longs for You in a dry and thirsty land where there is no water" (Psalm 63:1, NKJV).

"Blessed are those who hunger and thirst for righteousness, for they shall be filled" (Matthew 5:6, NKJV).

Adapted by permission from E.M. Bounds, Prayer and Revival *(Baker Book House).*

Chapter 9

Why Pastors Need Intercession

by Dr. C. Peter Wagner

━━━━◆◆◆━━━━

I am convinced that most church members have little or no appreciation of the cost of being a pastor. They know what their pastor looks like and sounds like on the outside, but they have little more idea of what is happening on the inside than they have about what is happening on the inside of the digital watch they look at many times a day.

If God is going to raise up a new army of intercessors who will support pastors and other Christian leaders in effective, fervent prayer, these intercessors need to know both the scope and the urgency of the task ahead of them. I am going to be as frank as I possibly can in this chapter, but I do not want to be sensational.

This is not a column for the *National Enquirer*. Nothing I say about pastors and other leaders is to be taken as critical any more than a doctor diagnosing hepatitis or high blood pressure is critical of the patient. My purpose is healing. I believe that intercession cannot only be therapeutic for pastors' spiritual and emotional maladies, but much more importantly, I believe prayer can be preventative.

Pastors Are Beat Up

The pastor most church members see, know, and relate to over a period of time conforms to a well-established social role model. Certain things are expected of a pastor that are not necessarily expected of an automobile mechanic or a lawyer. The title "Reverend" carries strong social connotations.

29

Church members tend to take this for granted. Not pastors! Pastors are constantly at work projecting a suitable image for a clergy person. They are trained to do this in seminary and Bible school. It does not come naturally.

The pastors church members seek week in and week out are on their best behavior. They are appropriately dressed, they have a cheerful disposition, they are affirming, they do not lose their temper, they watch their language, they treat their spouses well, they are unselfish, they work hard, they keep smiling, and they hope their people see them as Christlike. But this is only part of the story.

Pastors are also human beings. They are saved by grace, but they are saved and sanctified no differently from the auto mechanics and lawyers in their congregations. Many, if not most, pastors will actually remind their people of this in their sermons from time to time.

When pastors talk about a certain temptation, for example, they might say, "I am not exempting myself; I am human. This is as much of a temptation for me as it is for you." The people usually acknowledge this as an honest appraisal. But they do not really believe it, mainly because they don't want to. Part of their own Christian well-being depends to a degree on following a pastoral leader whom they regard as somewhat higher on the scale of piety and spiritual attainment than they might ever be. Using society's help, they often put their pastor on a spiritual pedestal.

Pastors are also trained not to be hypocrites. They know very well they are not all their congregations expect them to be. Their spouses know this, too, but few others do. Consequently, pastors are caught in a bind, for they sense God's calling on their lives to be pastors, and they know they cannot do an effective job as pastors if they don't outwardly conform to their congregations' expectations. But how do they handle what is going on inside?

In a word, pastors need help—at least more help than they have been getting. In the course of a year, I meet and interact with hundreds of pastors. Even though I don't relate to them as a counselor or a pastor to pastors, I find that many are beat up—spiritually, emotionally, and sometimes physically.

Where can they go for help? They are reluctant to go to any of their church members, for the word could too easily leak out: Our pastor is failing us by not conforming to our expectations. Pastors in the same denomination are usually on friendly terms with one another but somewhat distrustful at the deeper levels. What would church members think if their pastor were seeing a professional counselor? Pastors of other churches in the same community are likely prospects for help, but they're frequently overburdened and unavailable. Beyond those circles, most pastors simply run out of meaningful relationships.

Happily, there are some exceptions. A fair number of pastors do not fit this bleak picture I'm painting. They have little internal conflict because deep down they actually are what they are expected to be emotionally and spiritually. Some are not, but they have found sources of help and are managing their situation well. I wish I could report that these are in the majority, but I'm afraid I can't. Without wanting to oversimplify a complex situation, I do want to point out that Satan has many pastors just where he wants them. They are vulnerable to his attacks.

Our Epidemic of Falling Pastors

Over the past couple of decades, an alarming number of pastors have dropped out of the ministry for two main reasons: pastoral burnout and sexual immorality. The numbers have reached epidemic proportions.

I can't remember hearing about pastoral burnout 20 years ago. It must have existed, but not to the degree we see it today. The situation I have described, resulting in pastors' being so beaten up, makes it easy to understand why so much burnout would occur. The enemy knows this well and has become astute at raising frustrations through feelings of inadequacy, hypocrisy, guilt, and low self-esteem to such levels that selling insurance can seem to some a more-attractive way to make a living.

A good bit of psychological research is currently being done on causes and remedies for pastoral burnout. Good time-management training is helping many to avoid it. Nevertheless, if I'm correct in suspecting that the powers of darkness are also at work in causing burnout, spiritual weapons are also needed. This is where intercession for pastors has enormous potential.

Pastoral Indiscretion

Satan wins significant battles by causing pastoral burnout, but he inflicts immeasurably more damage to the cause of Christ when he influences a pastor to fall through sexual immorality.

Before I go into more detail on this delicate subject, let me just remind us that most American pastors have never fallen into sexual immorality while in the ministry, nor will they. In fact, approximately 9 out of 10 have had no overt problems in this area, which by comparison is only half the percentage of other church members who have had similar problems. How many have gone all the way? A survey by the clergy journal *Leadership* found that 12 percent of pastors have actually committed adultery (winter quarter 1988, pp. 12-13; the "9 out of 10" is my extrapolation from the data reported). This means 88 percent have not.

Surveys like this would never have been dreamed of a generation ago. Elmer Gantry was not looked upon as a realistic prototype of anything but a minuscule fringe of American clergy. Today the picture has changed. I've been filing news items in a folder I never looked back into until now. I'm appalled at what I find. I count 26 media reports of sexual immorality on the part of high-profile clergy, almost half of whom I know personally.

A front-page article in the *Los Angles Times* carries the headline "Sex Abuse Cases Rock the Clergy: Disclosures of misconduct—a problem hidden for years—are on the rise." A nationally syndicated column by the Associated Press announces that "sex scandals in higher ranks shake up hierarchies."

Evangelicals, charismatics, fundamentalists, Pentecostals, liberals, and Roman Catholics all wish they could point their fingers at the others, but none is exempt. Here is a mainline bishop, known widely as an evangelical. Here is a seminary professor. Here is a televangelist. Here is a civil rights folk hero. Here is a megachurch pastor. Here is a best-selling author. Here is a missions leader. Here is a liberation theologian. Here is a black; there is a white. Here is a 25-year-old; there is a 60-year-old. Here is a pastor from Massachusetts; there is a pastor from Arizona. Where is it going to stop?

Reporting this makes me angry! I'm not angry at my friends who have fallen even though I, along with the rest of the Body of Christ, have been harmed. I'm angry at the enemy who, I feel, is getting away with far too much these days. We often fail to recognize the depth of the spiritual battle we are fighting.

The enemy knows pastors are beat up; he knows they are vulnerable, and he attacks them at their weakest point. This is not to say that those who have fallen are not themselves guilty and don't have character flaws that need to be repaired through humility, repentance, reconciliation, restoration, and holiness. But I do hope and pray we will learn how to use our spiritual weapons more effectively in putting a stop to these blatant and all-too-successful attacks of the devil against them.

Pastors Need Intercession

Every Christian needs intercession. The little girl in the sixth grade learning what AIDS means needs intercession. The long-haul truck driver trying to witness to his friends about Jesus needs intercession. The Christian stockbroker wrestling with the ethics of that last deal needs intercession. The mother and homemaker raising a family of four needs intercession. I don't want to ignore the need for more-consistent ministries of intercession across the board.

I do want to argue, however, that pastors and other Christian leaders need intercession more than ordinary members of the Body of Christ. This may sound strange and even arrogant at first, but let me propose five reasons why I believe it to be true.

1.   *Pastors have more responsibility and accountability.*
Most Christian leaders get chills up and down their
spines when they read James 3:1:"My brethren, let not
many of you become teachers, knowing that we shall
receive a stricter judgment" (NKJV). All Christians will
come before the judgment seat of Christ, but pastors
and other leaders have been forewarned that there's a
divine double standard, one for "teachers" and one for all
the rest.

In other words, in the eyes of God, a given sin is
worse for a pastor to commit than for others. The first
problem, of course, is the sin itself, and that may be
the same for everyone. But the second problem is the
violation of the office, which is even more serious.
When an office such as pastor or teacher (including
seminary professor) has been granted by God and
recognized by the Christian community, it is a griev-
ous offense to break that trust.

Accepting a position of leadership in the Christian
world is running a risk. Sin becomes more dangerous
than ever before. And this is one reason pastors have a
greater need for intercession.

2.   *Pastors are more subject to temptation.*
Make no mistake about it, the higher up you go on the
ladder of Christian leadership, the higher you go on
Satan's hit list. The devil is characterized as a roaring
lion seeking whom he may devour. If he has a choice,
he will devour a leader before he will devour anyone
else. And he will use every weapon in his arsenal to
do it.

Satan uses the world (Ephesians 2:1-2). He tempts
pastors with greed and power and pride. Money and
power team up with sex as some of the strongest
lures for ministers. It took recent investigative reporting by the secular media to uncover some of the
greed among Christian leaders, which others of us
have not particularly wanted to face. And I believe
more alarming news is to come. The love of money is

the root of evil, and Satan has been getting in at that point more than some have suspected.

Satan uses the flesh (Ephesians 2:2-3). Enough has been said about illicit sex. Satan also perverts the mind with pornography. Other ministers are tempted to fall into gluttony or alcohol and substance abuse.

Satan also uses "the devil" (1 Peter 5:8; compare John 13:27). This means demonization, spells, curses, and incantations. To imagine that pastors are only subject to the world and the flesh, but not evil forces, is in itself a clear satanic deception.

It's true that all Christians are subject to all of the above. But Satan is more specific, persistent, and intentional when it comes to pastors and other leaders.

3.   *Pastors are more targeted by spiritual warfare.*
It has now become known that over the last several years, satanists, witches, New Agers, occult practitioners, shamans, spiritists, and other servants of darkness have entered into an evil covenant to pray to Satan for the breakdown of marriages of pastors and Christian leaders. The spiritual warfare has intensified.

In my book *Warfare Prayer,* I distinguish three levels of spiritual warfare: (1) ground-level spiritual warfare, which is ordinary deliverance ministry; (2) occult-level spiritual warfare, which involves spells and curses by spiritual practitioners of darkness; and (3) strategic-level spiritual warfare, which deals with territorial principalities and powers. All three levels interact with one another to varying degrees, but the warfare is different in each case. Here I am dealing with the middle, or occult, level of spiritual warfare. Special kinds of intercessors are needed to deal with this most effectively, and other intercessors are needed as backup.

Spiritual warfare is such an important issue that I want to be sure we don't just think it's a figment of someone's imagination. I have personal correspondence from two respected Christian leaders who have had firsthand exposure to this. They help us understand the reality of the struggle we have been drawn into.

The first report is from John Vaughan of the International Mega-Church Research Center and Southwest Baptist University in Bolivar, Missouri. The scenario of his report is an airplane flight from Detroit to Boston, where Vaughan was to do a pastors' seminar.

John had not conversed with or paid much attention to the man in the seat next to him until he saw the man bow his head and move his lips as if praying. When he finished, John asked, "Are you a Christian?" The man had no way of knowing that Vaughan himself was a Christian, a Baptist pastor, and a university professor.

The man seemed shocked by the question and said, "Oh, no. You have me all wrong. I'm not a Christian, I'm actually a satanist!"

John asked him what he was praying for as a satanist. He said, "Do you really want to know?"

When John said he did, the satanist replied, "My primary attention is directed toward the fall of Christian pastors and their families living in New England." He asked John what he was going to do in Boston.

John reports, "After a brief conversation about my ministry and its purposes for the kingdom of God, he indicated that he needed to return to his work!"

John Vaughan says that encounter made him realize just how essential intercession for pastors really is. Did Christians take time to pray for their pastors in New England that day? Whose prayer was answered—the Christians' or the satanists'?

The second correspondence was from Bill McRae, the chancellor of two prestigious evangelical institutions near Toronto, Canada—Ontario Bible College and Ontario Theological Seminary. Previously he pastored the North Park Community Chapel in London, Ontario.

He reports that while he was a pastor, "it was brought to our attention that a group of satanists who worshipped in a church situation within London had committed themselves to pray to Satan for the elimination of a number of our evangelical leaders in the city through marriage and family breakdown. During that summer, the cell group in London was honored at a particular satanist convention for being so effective and successful during that year."

Why did they win the award? McRae says, "In the course of the previous year, they had succeeded through their prayers to Satan in eliminating five of our very significant leading men from pastoral ministries through immorality and marriage breakdown!"

Bill McRae explains that he was deeply involved with one of the pastors who was going through this nightmarish and disgraceful fall from Christian ministry. He says, "We were very much aware of the desperate need for prayer, but I must frankly confess none of us was quite as alert to the reality of the satanic warfare we were fighting until it was all over. "

McRae also tells of a group of his friends who went into a restaurant in London and observed a prayer meeting in a corner booth. They introduced themselves as fellow Christians, but the pray-ers quickly identified themselves as members of the church of Satan in London. They admitted (bragged?) that they had been praying that night specifically to Satan for the destruction of a certain pastor. McRae says, "They mentioned his name, and he is a very good friend of mine in one of the leading churches in London. It once again brought home to me the dark reality of the satanic battle in which we are engaged."

Another aspect of the satanic attack pastors are under is a demonic spirit of lust. Let me give you an example of what I mean. In a recent two-week Doctor of Ministry course, I said something that sounded humorous when it came out of my mouth. Here I had 50 pastors from across the denominational spectrum and from many different parts of the country. On the first day of class I mentioned that my wife, Doris, who is also my secretary and to whom many of them had talked on the phone, has had a powerful ministry of praying for pastors one-on-one and has helped them a great deal. I casually told them that she has a particularly effective track record of delivering pastors from demonic spirits of lust. Then I said, "So if any of you have a problem with lust, go see my wife!"

I said it so spontaneously and naively that we all burst out in laughter. But then what happened? No fewer than six of them made appointments with Doris for deliverance sessions! They went home with a new lease on life. Several wrote back or called to tell Doris how different and more enjoyable life has been since they were delivered from those foul spirits. One wrote, "For the first time since we have been married, my wife and I can now pray together. "

Nothing said here should cause us to suppose that demonization relieves pastors or others of moral responsibility. The roots of the activity of the spirit of lust can be traced, more often than not, to the "lusts of the flesh" (see 1 John 2:16) or sin that needs to be identified and dealt with biblically. Part and parcel of the deliverance process is typically (1) a personal recognition of and hatred for the sin; (2) a sincere desire to get rid of it; (3) a courageous first step of faith, like making an appointment to see Doris; and (4) confession of the sin, frequently in considerable detail.

This fulfills James 5:16: "Confess your trespasses to one another, and pray for one another, that you may be healed" (NKJV). In this case, the healing is spiritual. Upon sincere repentance, the root sin is forgiven by God's grace, and the legal grounds of the subsequent demonic activity are effectively removed. Once this is accomplished, the demonic spirit can be cast out relatively easily. Without sincere humility and repentance, however, the demon either stays or soon returns with reinforcements.

I have dealt with this subject of spiritual warfare in some detail for two reasons. First, I want to make sure we understand that it is real. It's certainly not the only cause, but I would not be surprised if it were a major cause of so many pastors' falling into sexual immorality.

Second, I want us to understand that there is a remedy, namely the power of God released through effective, intelligent intercession in the name of Jesus. My burden is to explain how this power can be released for repairing the damage already done by the enemy and preventing future occurrences.

4.   *Pastors have more influence on others.*
The fourth reason pastors need intercession more than other Christians is that by the very nature of their ministry, they have more influence on others. If a pastor falls, more people are set back in their spiritual lives than if others fall. The ripple effect is incredibly devastating. Strong Christians are crushed by the hypocrisy and betrayal they feel. Weak Christians take the pastor's behavior as a license for them to do likewise.

Not only does the fall of the pastor injure an untold number of people, but it also directly influences churches. My interest in church growth always focuses strongly on the pastor because we have evidence that the pastor is the major institutional factor for determining the growth or nongrowth of a local church. Satan hates churches that glorify God and extend God's kingdom, and he does what he can to bring them down. No wonder he focuses his sights on pastors.

But in the plan of God, the gates of hell will not prevail against the advance of the church (see Matthew 16:18). Intercession for pastors is one important ingredient to release God's plan for the church's fullest implementation.

5.   *Pastors have more visibility.*
Because pastors are up front, they are constantly subject to gossip and criticism. When church members have Sunday dinner, the pastor and the sermon of the morning are frequent topics of conversation. People talk about the good and also the bad. The pastor is closely observed, and it's no secret. Just knowing this places a difficult burden on pastors, and they need supernatural

help to handle that situation well. Intercession opens the way for them to receive this help.

Intercession Improves Ministry

It is not a simple matter to conduct research that proves or disproves the power of prayer. However, Nancy Pfaff, an intercessor, church-growth consultant, and founder of Nevada Church Growth, has attempted it. She designed a research instrument and surveyed 130 pastors, evangelists, and missionaries. Intercessors trained through Iverna Tompkins Ministries of Scottsdale, Arizona, agreed to pray 15 minutes a day for one of the 130 leaders over an entire year.

About 89 percent of those surveyed indicated that the prayer had caused a positive change in their ministry effectiveness. They reported more effectiveness in the use of their particular spiritual gifts, a higher level of positive response to their ministry, more discernment and wisdom from God, increased wholeness in Christ, improved attitudes, more evidence of the fruit of the Spirit, better personal prayer lives, and heightened leadership skills.

Pfaff's research also uncovered important variables. She found that daily prayer for leaders was more effective than weekly or monthly prayer. Also, persistent prayer was shown to be important. She reports, "Where intercessors stopped praying for their assigned leader after a few weeks, the leaders indicated no significant positive change in their lives and ministries during that year" (*Journal of the North American Society for Church Growth,* 1990 edition, p. 82).

Intercession also seems to help church growth. Nancy Pfaff found that of 109 pastors covered by intercessory prayer, 60 percent indicated simultaneous growth of their churches. A pastor from Pennsylvania testified, for example, that in the 12-month prayer experiment period, his church grew from 15 to more than 600. No wonder Pfaff says, "There exists a tremendous reservoir of untapped prayer power in every church which can be affirmed, trained, and deployed to see the lost won, the apathetic revived, the 'backslider' restored, and the committed made more effective" (Ibid., p. 83).

Back when the well-known Evangelism Explosion (EE) program was moving out from Coral Ridge Presbyterian Church in Fort Lauderdale, Florida, and spreading across the country, Archie Parrish, who was then serving as director, made an important discovery. Even though the program was working well, he introduced a new innovation. He had each participating church enlist two members who were not in the EE program to pray for each EE worker, especially on the Tuesday nights when the program was in operation. The evangelist was responsible to report back to his or her two intercessors each week. Parrish found that when intercessors prayed, the number of professions of faith doubled!

Pastors and other Christian leaders are needy people. But they are God's chosen ones to move His kingdom forward. Faithful and intelligent intercession can release them to be all God wants them to be.

Adapted by permission from Dr. C. Peter Wagner, Prayer Shield *(www.arsenalbooks.com)*.

Chapter 10

How to Pray for Your Pastor and His Family

———◆•◆———

W
e should have this general attitude in praying for our pastors:

> Therefore encourage one another, and build up one another, just as you also are doing. But we request of you, brethren, that you appreciate those who diligently labor among you, and have charge over you in the Lord and give you instruction, and that you esteem them very highly in love because of their work. Live in peace with one another. (1 Thessalonians 5:11-13, NASB)

> I thank my God in all my remembrance of you, always offering prayer with joy in my every prayer for you all, in view of your participation in the gospel. (Philippians 1:3-5, NASB)

Note: You can pray the following scriptures for your own pastor by putting his name (or his family member's name) into the verses where appropriate.

What to Pray For

His relationship with God
- That he would be a man after God's own heart. *"… a man after My heart, who will do all My will"* (Acts 13:22, NASB). *"As the deer pants for the water brooks, so my soul pants for Thee, O God"* (Psalm 42:1, NASB).

- That he would be a man of the Word. *"O how I love Thy law! It is my meditation all the day"* (Psalm 119:97, NASB). *"Let the word of Christ richly dwell within you, with all wisdom teaching and admonishing one another with psalms and hymns and spiritual songs, singing with thankfulness in your hearts to God"* (Colossians 3:16, NASB). *"Thy word I have treasured in my heart, that I may not sin against Thee"* (Psalm 119:11, NASB).
- That he would allow the Lord to guide his every step. *"The steps of a man are established by the LORD"* (Psalm 37:23, NASB).
- That he would experience a growing and deepening relationship with the Lord in prayer. *"Delight yourself in the LORD; and He will give you the desires of your heart"* (Psalm 37:4, NASB). *"O God, Thou art my God; I shall seek Thee earnestly; my soul thirsts for Thee, my flesh yearns for Thee, in a dry and weary land where there is no water. ... My soul clings to Thee; Thy right hand upholds me"* (Psalm 63:1,8, NASB).
- That he would be a Spirit-filled man of faith and love. *"For this reason, I bow my knees before the Father ... that He would grant you ... to be strengthened with power through His Spirit in the inner man; so that Christ may dwell in your hearts through faith; and that you, being rooted and grounded in love, may be able to comprehend ... and to know the love of Christ which surpasses knowledge, that you may be filled up to all the fulness of God"* (Ephesians 3:14-19, NASB).
- That the Lord will give him good health, strength, and endurance.

His family relationships
- That those relationships would be loving, unselfish, respectful, understanding, honoring, guiding, and harmonious. *"Husbands, love your wives, just as Christ also loved the church and gave Himself up for her"* (Ephesians 5:25, NASB). *"You husbands likewise, live with your wives in an understanding way"* (1 Peter 3:7a, NASB). *"Nevertheless let each individual among you also love his own wife even as*

himself; and let the wife see to it that she respect her husband" (Ephesians 5:33, NASB). *"Children, obey your parents in the Lord.... Honor your father and mother"* (Ephesians 6:1-2, NASB). *"Fathers, do not provoke your children to anger; but bring them up in the discipline and instruction of the Lord"* (Ephesians 6:4, NASB).

* That the family members would be a source of joy and blessing to one another. *"The father of the righteous will greatly rejoice, and he who begets a wise son will be glad in him"* (Proverbs 23:24, NASB). *"A woman who fears the* LORD, *she shall be praised.... Her children rise up and bless her; her husband also, and he praises her"* (Proverbs 31:30b, 28, NASB). *"A righteous man who walks in his integrity—how blessed are his sons after him"* (Proverbs 20:7, NASB).

* That God will protect his family, giving them good health, plus His joy and peace in all circumstances.

His ministry

* That he would be devoted to prayer and the ministry of the Word. *"But we will devote ourselves to prayer, and to the ministry of the word"* (Acts 6:4, NASB).

* That he would intercede for his people in prayer and instruct them.

* That he would know the hearts and needs of his people and be able to pray for and minister to them accordingly. *"Moreover, as for me, far be it from me that I should sin against the* LORD *by ceasing to pray for you; but I will instruct you in the good and right way"* (1 Samuel 12:23, NASB). *"For God ... is my witness as to how unceasingly I make mention of you, always in my prayers ..."* (Romans 1:9, 10a, NASB).

* That he would have a fruitful ministry. *"You did not choose Me, but I chose you, and appointed you, that you should go and bear fruit, and that your fruit should remain, that whatever you ask of the Father in My name, He may give to you"* (John 15:16, NASB). *"And we proclaim Him, admonishing every man and teaching every man with all wisdom, that we may present every man complete in Christ"* (Colossians 1:28, NASB).

- That he will be able to handle, with grace and patience, his many responsibilities.
- That he will be sensitive to the leading of the Lord both as he prepares and as he preaches, resulting in the Holy Spirit's speaking to the church through the message.
- That he will have a strong, close, harmonious working relationship with those in leadership.
- That the Lord will give him insights into the solutions for problems.
- That he will know how to counsel those who come to him for advice and help.
- That he would equip the saints for service and discipleship. *"And He gave some as ... pastors and teachers, for the equipping of the saints for the work of service, to the building up of the body of Christ"* (Ephesians 4:11-12, NASB). *"And the things which you have heard from me in the presence of many witnesses, these entrust to faithful men, who will be able to teach others also"* (2 Timothy 2:2, NASB).
- That he would be protected from the evil one. *"Finally, brethren, pray for us that the word of the Lord may spread rapidly and be glorified ... that we may be delivered from perverse and evil men; for not all have faith. But the Lord is faithful, and He will strengthen and protect you from the evil one"* (2 Thessalonians 3:1-3, NASB).

The church family's relationship with him and his family
- That the congregation will pray regularly for him and his family.
- That the congregation will respect and guard, as much as possible, his time with his family, especially in the early mornings, evenings, and weekends (i.e., not interrupting them unless absolutely necessary).
- That the congregation will not impose on his children standards that they do not expect other children to meet (i.e., that they will give them freedom to be kids).

Chapter 11

Scripture-Based Prayers to Pray for Your Pastor

1.   I thank You, Father, that Your eyes are on my shepherd, Your ears are attentive to his prayers, and Your face is against those who plot evil against him (1 Peter 3:12). For I know that in all things You work for the good of _____ (insert your pastor's name), who loves you (Romans 8:28). Who can accuse this pastor who daily is interceded for by Christ Jesus (Romans 8:33-34)? Therefore, in all things my pastor is more than a conqueror (Romans 8:37). Thank You, God.

2.   Lord, I pray for discernment in exposing any schemes of the enemy against my pastor. Show our congregation how to pray against all powers of this dark world and the spiritual forces of darkness in heavenly realms. And Lord, protect us as we wage warfare on behalf of our pastor (Ephesians 6:11-12).

3.   Father, I thank You that no weapons formed against my pastor will prosper. Every tongue raised against my shepherd will be cast down. Rumors and gossip will be turned aside. For _____ will be still before You, Lord, and wait on You. My pastor will dwell in the shadow of the Most High God and will be delivered from terror, darts of doubt, and diseases (Psalm 91:5-6). Set Your angels about my pastor (Psalm 91:11) and no power of the enemy shall harm _____ (Luke 10:19). Thank God forevermore!

4.   Lord, let _____ have a discerning mind to prioritize the precious minutes in the day. Let my pastor understand

what is most important and be guarded against the
tyranny of the urgent (Psalm 90:12).

5.   Father, inspire my pastor to glory only in the cross
(Galatians 6:14). Keep my pastor from pride or self-
pity. Let the cross be his reason for ministry.

6.   Jesus, keep my pastor holy in every way (1 Peter 1:15-
16). Protect my shepherd from seducing spirits, especially when he is tired and hard-pressed. Give _____
comrades to help protect him and encourage him in
personal holiness (Ecclesiastes 4:12). As my pastor
draws near to You, draw near to my pastor (James 4:8).

7.   I pray that the eyes of my pastor may be enlightened
to know the hope to which we are called and the riches
of our glorious inheritance as saints. Let my pastor
know the incomparably great power which is in us who
believe (Ephesians 1:18-19). Let _____ see the full
revelation of Jesus Christ (Galatians 1:12). Place in him a
desire to know Christ and the power of His resurrection
(Philippians 3:10).

8.   Lord, I lift up the hands of my pastor and his family.
Place them in the shelter of the Most High to rest in the
shadow of the Almighty. I will say of the Lord, You are
their refuge and fortress. You will preserve their family
time. You will cover their home. Your faithfulness will
meet their financial needs in Christ Jesus (Philippians
4:19). You will command Your angels to guard them as
they travel and win the lost. You have said, "I will be
with [them] in trouble; I will deliver [them] and honor
[them]. With long life I will satisfy [them], and show
[them] My salvation" (Psalm 91:15-16, NKJV). In Jesus'
name I reject all attacks of the enemy against them.

9.   In Jesus' name I pray for church hurts, abuse, and
ungrateful forces to move. I call for mountains of criticism and inordinate expectations to be cast into the sea.

I pray that stress, excessive demands, and fatigue would be relieved, and I believe every need, vision, and dream of _____'s will be completed (Mark 11:22-24; Philippians 4:19).

10.   Forgive those who hurt _____ and speak against him, and may my pastor walk in forgiveness (Ephesians 4:32—5:1). Guard my pastor from futile thinking (Ephesians 4:17) and vain imagination. Let every thought be taken captive to obey Christ (2 Corinthians 10:3-5).

11.   In Jesus' name I bind the fear of failure and the fear of humankind (John 14:1). Let _____'s confidence not be eroded by the daily resistance to the gospel that he encounters. Encourage my pastor to fear God more than people.

12.   Father, heal my shepherd's heart of any grief caused by ministry. Bestow on him a crown of beauty instead of ashes, and anoint him with the oil of gladness instead of mourning. Clothe my shepherd with a garment of praise instead of a spirit of depression. I call my pastor an oak of righteousness, a planting of the Lord to display Your splendor (Isaiah 61:3).

13.   Keep my pastor in the midst of good and exciting worship. Keep him from the traditions of men and religion that hold a form of godliness but deny its power (2 Timothy 3:5). Give _____ a vision of heaven (Isaiah 6; Revelation 4).

14.   With my shield of faith I cover my shepherd's mind to quench all flaming darts of doubt, vain imagination, or mental distractions (Ephesians 6:16; Colossians 2:6-8). Let the mind of Christ be strong in my pastor (1 Corinthians 2:16).

15.   Lord, I stand against the enemies of my pastor's
      prayer life: busyness, compulsions, compromise (Acts 5),
      unnecessary phone calls, chronic counselees, sleepiness
      (Matthew 26:40-41), appetites, television, late meetings,
      overcommitments, and doubt. Let nothing hinder_____'s
      time with You. Let my pastor rise up to seek You (Mark
      1:35), pray with other pastors (Acts 1:14), and pray with
      out ceasing (1 Thessalonians 5:17). Give my pastor the
      time, the desire, and the place to pray (Acts 16:13). I
      rebuke in the name of Jesus any distractions from my
      pastor's devotional life.

16.   Bless my pastor with a rich study time (Acts 6:4; 2
      Timothy 2:15).

17.   As _____ preaches, let him proclaim Jesus Christ
      (Colossians 1:28). Let my pastor's preaching be in the
      energy of the Holy Spirit.

18.   Lord, by Your Holy Spirit, anoint _____ to preach.
      Let the oppressed be set free. Let people be cut to the
      heart and put their faith in Jesus Christ.

19.   Lord, as You have promised, grant my beloved shep-
      herd lasting fruit (Malachi 3:11; John 15:16). Let my
      pastor's converts become disciples who in turn bless
      my pastor with disciples who grow in the grace and
      knowledge of Jesus Christ.

20.   Lord, keep my pastor in the fear of God (Proverbs
      19:23). Give _____ boldness to confront sin and
      church controllers. Honor his stand for You. Come to
      his rescue. I claim Psalm 35 for my shepherd.

Adapted by permission from Terry Teykl, Your Pastor:
Preyed On or Prayed For, *Prayer Point Press, Inc.*

Chapter 12

Strategic Prayer Plan

G od expects us to pray for our leaders, in government and elsewhere. We are to pray that they will be capable people who fear God. God answers the prayers of His people. In 2 Chronicles 7:14, God promises He will heal our land if we seek His face and turn from our wicked ways. "Blessed is the nation whose God is the LORD" (Psalm 33:12, NASB).

Prayer is also the most-powerful way in which we can help our families and those around us in our communities.

Praying for Our Government

People to pray for:
President of the United States: George Bush
Vice President of the United States: Dick Cheney
Secretary of State: Colin Powell
Secretary of Defense: Donald Rumsfeld
Secretary of Treasury: Paul O'Neill
Attorney General: John Ashcroft
Secretary of the Interior: Gale Norton
Secretary of Agriculture: Ann Veneman
Secretary of Commerce: Don Evans
Secretary of Labor: Elaine Chao
Secretary of Transportation: Norman Mineta
Secretary of Energy: Spencer Abraham
Secretary of Education: Rod Paige
Secretary of Veterans Affairs: Anthony Principi
Secretary of Health and Human Services: Tommy Thompson
Secretary of Housing and Urban Development: Mel
    Martinez
Surgeon General: David Satcher
Speaker of the U.S. House of Representatives

Majority leaders of the U.S. Senate and House of Represen-
tatives
Minority leaders of the Senate and House
Cabinet members
Leaders of the White House staff
U.S. senators, especially those from your state
U.S. representatives, especially those from your state
Chaplains of the U.S. Senate and House of Representatives
U.S. Supreme Court
All branches of the armed forces
Governor of your state
State senators and representatives from your state
Elected and top appointed leaders from your community:
  Mayor, city and county officials, judges, police and fire
    departments
  Schools: teachers, administrators, and officials

Issues to pray about:
• Wisdom and courage in decisions involving Christian
  issues
• Government restraint in issues regarding Christian homes
  and families
• Wisdom regarding issues of education and moral values

Praying for the Church

Your pastor, associate pastors, youth leaders, worship leaders
Other church leaders for whom God leads you to pray:
  • Elders, deacons, church officers, secretaries, Sunday school
    teachers, Bible study groups, nursery helpers, choir mem-
    bers, ushers
Leaders of all Christian organizations:
  • Ask God to help them stand strong in their convictions
    and be bold in their witness.
National events like Promise Keepers, National Day of
  Prayer, Concerts of Prayer
Prisoners and prison ministries
Evangelists, ministers, and other leaders who speak to large
  audiences

Television and radio ministers
Those responsible for publishing Christian books,
magazines, etc.

Praying for the Media

- That they would reflect godly values in their coverage
- That they would be accurate and fair in their presentations
- That they would place a high value on truth and decency

Praying for Your Family and Families in General

- Blessings and prosperity
- That they would serve one another in love
- That they would be dedicated to one another

Praying for the Fatherless

- Pray that God would burden your heart for a fatherless child.
- Pray that God would lead your church to reach out to hurting children.

Praying for the Last, the Lost, and the Least

- Pray for a burden for all people.
- Pray that your church would become a lighthouse for the lost.
- Pray that God would use you to reach the homeless, hungry, and hurting.

Chapter 13

Front-Lines Praying

―――◆◆◆――――

"Finally, my brethren, be strong in the Lord and in the power of His might. Put on the whole armor of God" (Ephesians 6:10-11, NKJV). "For the weapons of our warfare are not carnal [of the flesh] but mighty in God for pulling down strongholds, casting down arguments and every high thing that exalts itself against the knowledge of God, bringing every thought into captivity to the obedience of Christ" (2 Corinthians 10:4-5, NKJV).

As those scriptures indicate, we're in a battle. If we choose to be on the front lines of that battle, we need to know how to be safe from enemy attacks. Part of that is being aware of the areas the enemy likes to attack in order to weaken and defeat us or put us on the sidelines for a while. The enemy will try to knock us out any way he can. "[He] walks about like a roaring lion, seeking whom he may devour" (1 Peter 5:8, NKJV). If we're to be front-lines warriors, we need to stay alert, be watchful, and arm ourselves, putting on the whole armor of God.

Our God-given Weapons for Warding Off Enemy Attack

- Practice personal confession and dedication (Psalm 19:12-14; Proverbs 28:13).
- Resist all temptation (Luke 22:40; 1 Corinthians 10:13).
- Desire purity and holiness (Leviticus 20:7; Ephesians 1:4).
- Practice humility (Philippians 2:3; James 4:10; 1 Peter 5:5).
- Establish praise and worship as a way of life (Psalms 103; 104; 105).
- Ask to know the Lord's agenda for your life (Psalm 25:4-5).
- Keep your eyes on the Lord, not on circumstances, no matter how difficult it gets (Proverbs 3:5-6).

- Ask the Lord to give you vision and to help you see things from His perspective.
- Keep an optimistic spirit (Philippians 4:4-8).
- Take quality time to be alone with the Lord and listen to Him (Psalm 46:10). One of the first things the enemy tries to do is to interfere with our quiet times by either eliminating them or getting us to rush through them. Ask the Lord to keep them fresh and meaningful so they draw you even closer to Him.
- Ask the Lord for good health, both physically and emotionally, for you and your family (Psalm 35:27; 103:3).
- Pray on the armor of God each morning as part of your preparation for the day's battle (Ephesians 6:11-17).

Winning Prayer Victories

Take the offensive in prayer.
- God called Moses to lead Israel out of the land of Egypt, not to defend them in Egypt; to attack and defeat the enemy nations, not to protect Israel from them.
- God sent Joshua to conquer Canaan, not to negotiate détente.
- The Holy Spirit was given at Pentecost, not to keep the church blessed and comfortable but to make the church invincible.
- The weapons of our spiritual warfare are not defensive weapons but weapons of attack (2 Corinthians 10:4-5).
- We are not to build a bypass when Satan throws up a mountain of resistance against us; we are to challenge Satan and hurl his mountain into the sea (Matthew 17:20).
- We are not to "hold the fort" till Jesus comes to rescue us; we are to storm "the gates of Hades." And God has promised they "shall not prevail against [us]" (Matthew 16:18, NKJV).
- Ask God to give you a bold spirit; ask Him to point out specific needs for which to pray. Ask Him to show you the blindness, the slavery, and the hopelessly lost condition of the unsaved.
- Ask God to give you a new joy and expectancy in prayer, a holy boldness to see Christ triumph and Satan defeated. Ask Him to clothe your prayer with the authority of Calvary, the

power of Pentecost, and the almightiness of His name.
- Ask God to light a holy fire in your soul by the power of the Holy Spirit, to transform your praying from weakness to prevailing power and an urgent insistence to see God's will done "on earth as it is in heaven."

Do everything in the power of the Holy Spirit.
- The Holy Spirit has come to drive out Satan before you: "Resist the devil and he will flee from you" (James 4:7, NKJV). "When the enemy comes in like a flood, the Spirit of the Lord will lift up a standard against him" (Isaiah 59:19, NKJV).
- If the Holy Spirit is filling you and leading you in your praying and you're invading Satan's territory to deliver his captives, the Holy Spirit is right there to clothe your words with Jesus' authority.
- In this warfare you do not fight alone; the battle belongs to the Lord. "Finally, my brethren, be strong in the Lord and in the power of His might" (Ephesians 6:10, NKJV). "Do not be afraid nor dismayed because of this great multitude, for the battle is not yours, but God's" (2 Chronicles 20:15, NKJV). "The LORD your God, who goes before you, He will fight for you" (Deuteronomy 1:30, NKJV).

In holy faith, resist and defeat Satan.
- A word of caution: Don't become devil-conscious. God is the Sovereign One, not Satan. Don't be absorbed with your enemy. Resist him when you need to; command him to go. But focus your eyes on Jesus, seated on the throne of heaven.
- Don't give the devil more credit than he deserves. There are situations the devil is now dominating that will not change until you take the offensive and drive him out.
- There are people enslaved by Satan who are unable to free themselves. They will remain in Satan's bondage until you or others of God's people drive back the darkness and force Satan to release them.
- Satan is a defeated foe. Jesus defeated him on Calvary! We claim that victory to break his power over us.

Saturate your soul with the Word of God.
- Be careful to maintain your spiritual strength at all times. "Take... the sword of the Spirit, which is the word of God" (Ephesians 6:17, NKJV).
- Commit the truths and promises of God's Word to memory. There's no better way to be transformed by the renewing of your mind (Romans 12:2) and to be prepared for whatever challenges may come your way.
- During prayer, quote the Bible and read the promises of God. Use one or two special promises that you can claim for victory.

Use praise as a weapon against the enemy.
- "Let the saints be joyful in glory; let them sing aloud on their beds. Let the high praises of God be in their mouth, and a two-edged sword in their hand, ... to bind their kings with chains, and their nobles with fetters of iron; to execute on them the written judgment—this honor have all His saints. Praise the LORD!" (Psalm 149:5-6, 8-9, NKJV).
- With God's Word, your double-edged sword (Hebrews 4:12), in your hand and God's praise on your lips, all the demons of hell will flee before you!

Principles of Interceding for Others in Prayer

- Before interceding, we must realize our own inability.
- Intercession helps us focus on God as the only supplier of our needs.
- Intercession is loving others through prayer.
- Intercession seeks God's supply on behalf of others.
- Intercession enables the pray-er to be a channel of God's blessings.
- Intercession involves us in spiritual warfare on behalf of others.

The Power of Prayer

Prayer should not be the Christian's last resort, *but the first.* When we begin to address a need by taking action, we employ our own wisdom and strength. *When we start with prayer, we enlist the wisdom and power of Almighty God.* As Alfred, Lord Tennyson wrote, "More things are wrought by prayer/than this world dreams of." Or as a wise believer put it, "A day without prayer is a day without blessing, and a life without prayer is a life without power." So let us accept God's gracious invitation to come to Him as a trusting child to a loving Father. Let's pray reverently, humbly, continually, expectantly, and gratefully.

When we pray that way, *the Lord will be pleased to hear and to answer, we will be blessed abundantly, and He will be glorified.* "Now to him who is able to do immeasurably more than all we ask or imagine, according to his power that is at work within us, to him be glory in the church and in Christ Jesus throughout all generations, for ever and ever! Amen" (Ephesians 3:20-21, NIV).

The Christian Soldier's Creed

2 Timothy 2:3: *"Endure hardship as a good soldier of Jesus Christ" (NKJV).*

Recognizing that I was chosen by God to be a soldier and accepting the hazards of spiritual warfare, I will always endeavor to uphold the prestige, honor, and glorious tradition of being a Christian warrior.

Acknowledging that a Christian soldier is commissioned to be a militant, a fighter, an aggressive warrior in the attack on the "gates of hell," I must also accept the fact that as a Christian soldier, my Commander in Chief expects me to engage the enemy on my knees, with the shout of victory, *"The battle belongs to the Lord!"*

Never shall I fail my brothers! I will always keep myself mentally alert, morally straight, and spiritually strong. I will shoulder more than my share of responsibility in every battle, whatever that may be.

Gallantly I will show the world that I'm a specially selected and well-trained soldier. My Christian demeanor, my readiness for battle, and the care of my equipment, the full armor of God, shall be an example for others to follow.

Energetically I will meet Your enemies upon my knees, Lord. My assigned post shall be the prayer closet. I shall defeat them on that field of battle, for I am continually training and will fight with all my might, remembering "Greater is He that is in me than he that is in the world." *Surrender* is not a Christian word! I will never leave a wounded brother to fall into the hands of the enemy, and under no circumstances will I ever embarrass my fellow warriors in Christ or my Commander in Chief.

Readily will I display the intestinal fortitude required to fight on to the Christian objective and complete my mission, even if I be the lone survivor, knowing that my Commander will "never leave me nor forsake me."

Untiringly will I defend the cause of my Commander, on my knees, at my post, knowing that "the prayer of a righteous man is powerful and effective."

Adapted by Dr. John Sparks from the U.S. Army Ranger's Creed